Vocabulary Readers

Amazing Apples

Jeff Bauer

SCHOLASTIC INC.

NEW YORK • TORONTO • LONDON • AUCKLAND • SYDNEY
MEXICO CITY • NEW DELHI • HONG KONG • BUENOS AIRES

ISBN: 0-439-87636-2

Photo Credits

Cover: Penny Tweedie/Stone/Getty Images; title page: Mark E. Gibson/DPA; contents page, top: Patti McConville/DPA; contents page, middle: Dwight Kuhn; contents page, bottom: Myrleen Ferguson Cate/PhotoEdit; page 4: David Young-Wolff/PhotoEdit; page 5: Adam Jones/DPA; page 6: Felicia Martinez/PhotoEdit; page 7, top: Patti McConville/DPA; page 7, bottom: Dwight Kuhn; page 8: Dwight Kuhn; page 9, both: Dwight Kuhn; page 10, top: Dwight Kuhn; page 10 bottom: John Kaprielian/Photo Researchers, Inc.; page 11, top: Mark E. Gibson/DPA; page 11, bottom: Dennis MacDonald/PhotoEdit; page 12: Richard Hamilton Smith/DPA; page 13: Vanessa Davies/Dorling Kindersley/Getty Images; page 14: David Young-Wolff/PhotoEdit; page 15: Myrleen Ferguson Cate/PhotoEdit; back cover: Patti McConville/DPA.

Photo research by Sarah Longacre
Design by Holly Grundon

12 11 10 9 8 7 6 7 8 9 10 11/0

Printed in the U.S.A.
First printing, September 2006

Contents

Chapter 1

All About Apples

Apples are crisp and round and juicy. Do you want to learn all about this amazing fruit? Read on!

Fun Fact

There are 7,500 kinds of apples in the world!

Apples come in many colors. There are green ones. There are yellow ones. And there are lots and lots of red ones!

An apple has different parts. The **stem** is on top. The **skin** covers the outside. An apple's skin helps to protect it.

Tiny seeds like these can grow into huge apple trees.

When you cut an apple in half it looks like this. The white part is called the **flesh**. The hard center is called the **core**. That is where you find the **seeds**.

Chapter 2

Apple Trees

Apples grow on trees. In winter, an apple tree rests. Sometimes the branches get covered with snow.

An apple tree's flowers are called apple blossoms.

In spring, an apple tree is thirsty. It drinks up all the rain that falls. The rain helps flowers grow on its branches.

This is a tiny apple.

In summer, the flowers turn into tiny apples. As the tree soaks up the sun, the apples grow and grow.

This is a ripe apple.

In fall, the apples are big and juicy. That means they are **ripe** and ready to pick.

Chapter 3

Eating Apples

There are many ways to enjoy apples. Apple pie is yummy! It is America's favorite kind of pie.

Fun Fact

Apples are also used to make jelly, muffins, breads, and cakes.

Applesauce is yummy! It is made from mashed up apples. That makes it easy for babies to eat.

Apple juice is yummy, too! The juice is squeezed out of apples. It takes about four apples to fill one glass.

Fun Fact

Apples are grown in every state in America.

But there is nothing like a plain apple! Why? It is shiny and sweet and simple to eat. Crunch, crunch, crunch!

Glossary

blossom (**bloss**-uhm): the flower on a fruit tree

core (**kor**): the hard center part of an apple

flesh (**flesh**): the white part of the apple that you eat

ripe (**ripe**): full grown and ready to eat

seed (**seed**): the tiny part of a plant from which new plants can grow

skin (**skin**): the outer layer of a fruit

stem (**stem**): the long main part of a plant from which flowers grow

Comprehension Questions

1. Can you name all the parts of an apple?
2. Can you share two facts about an apple tree?
3. Can you name three foods that come from apples?